3603548357

D0997246

A Dorling Kindersley Book

Project Editor Laura Buller
Editor Bridget Hopkinson
Art Editor Christopher Howson
Production Catherine Semark
Photography Pete Gardner

First published in Great Britain in 1992 by Dorling
Kindersley Publishers Limited, 9 Henrietta Street,
London WC2E 8PS
Reprinted 1994
Copyright © 1992 Dorling Kindersley Limited, London
Copyright © 1992 *text* Neil Ardley

All rights reserved. No part of this publication may be
reproduced, stored in a retrieval system, or transmitted
in any form or by any means, electronic, mechanical,
photocopying, recording or otherwise, without the
prior permission of the copyright owner.

WITHDR

A CIP catalogue record for this book is available
from the British Library

ISBN 0-86318-798-6

CR
531·
14
ARD

3603548357

Reproduced in Hong Kong by Bright Arts
Printed in Belgium by Proost

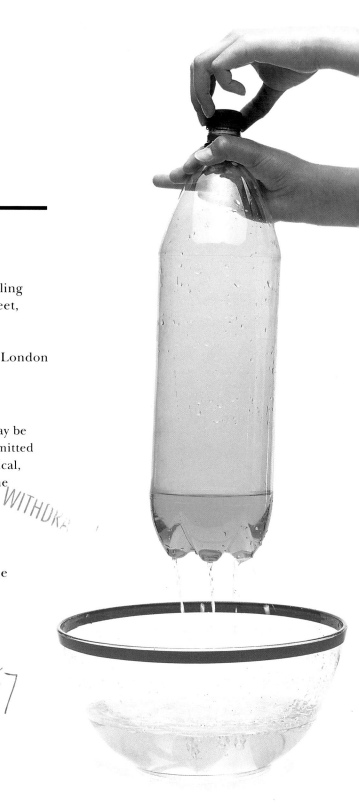

MY SCIENCE BOOK OF GRAVITY

Written by
Neil Ardley

DK

Dorling Kindersley
London • New York • Stuttgart

What is gravity?

When you jump up in the air, why do you fall back down again? You fall because of an invisible force called gravity. Gravity is a force that pulls objects together. It depends on mass, or the amount of matter that makes up an object. The larger the mass, the greater the pull. The Earth is so massive that its gravity is strong enough to pull everything on it towards its surface, and hold things there.

High dive
When this diver leaps off the diving board, gravity pulls him faster and faster towards the pool below.

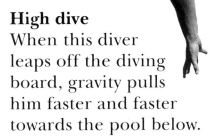

Watch your weight
Gravity pulls you downwards with a certain amount of force. This amount is your weight. You can measure it by standing on some scales.

Light work
The Moon has less mass than the Earth, so its gravity is much weaker. Astronauts have only a sixth of their normal weight when they are on the Moon, although their mass does not change.

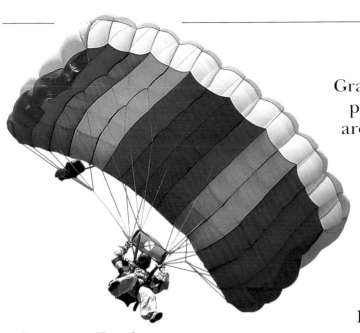

Held in space
Gravity keeps the planets in orbit around the Sun, and holds stars together in immense groups called galaxies.

Down to Earth
A parachute drops slowly because air pushes up on it, working against gravity.

Balance the ball
A sealion can balance a ball by keeping its nose under the ball's "centre of gravity", or balancing point.

Pulling power
Everything has gravity – even an apple pulls with a small force. But the Earth's pull is so much stronger that the apple falls down towards the ground.

⚠ This sign means **take care.** You should ask an adult to help you with this step of the experiment.

Be a safe scientist
Follow all the instructions and always be careful, especially when using scissors or sharp objects. Never put anything in your mouth or eyes.

When a step in an experiment requires you to swing things around or shoot them into the air, do it outside, in the open, away from other people.

Falling force

Does a heavy object fall faster than a light object? Drop a heavy ball and a light ball together and see which lands first. Discover how strongly gravity pulls on each ball.

You will need:

Ball bearing

Light plastic ball

Metal tray

Plasticine

Rolling pin

Make sure your hands are level when you drop the balls.

1 Weigh the two balls in your hands. The ball bearing should feel heavier. Put the tray on the ground.

2 Hold the two balls above the tray. Release them both at exactly the same time. Listen – you will hear them hit the tray together.

3 Roll out some plasticine.

The force of gravity makes everything fall at the same speed. The weight of an object makes no difference.

4 Place the plasticine on the tray. Then drop the two balls again so that they land on the plasticine.

The ball bearing makes the deepest dent, because gravity pulls on it with the strongest force.

5 Carefully lift up the balls to see which one has made the deepest dent in the plasticine.

Gravity pulls with more force on heavy objects than light objects. But heavy objects need more force to get them moving. So all objects fall at the same speed.

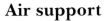

Air support

Very light objects, like these dandelion seeds, fall slowly or even float through the air. They are so light that the air holds them up, working against the force of gravity.

Hit the spot

Let go of some heavy and light balls at the top of a chute and try to guess exactly where they will land. How many of the balls do you think will land in the same place?

You will need:

Balls of different sizes

Plastic container

Cardboard box lid

Sticky tape

Scissors

Strip of card

Make one part bigger than the other.

1 Cut the lid into two parts. Then cut a half-circle in each part.

2 Cut tabs in each end of the strip of card.

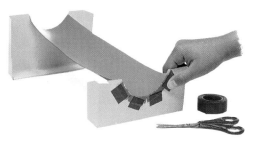

3 Fold back the tabs and tape them to the two parts of the lid to make a chute.

4 Raise the chute on a support. Let go of a ball at the top of the chute. Place the container where the ball lands.

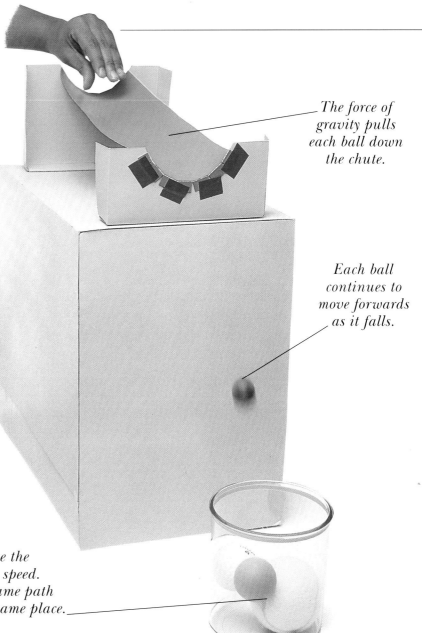

The force of gravity pulls each ball down the chute.

5 Let the balls go from the top of the chute one at a time. They all land in the container, even though the balls are different sizes!

Each ball continues to move forwards as it falls.

All the balls leave the chute at the same speed. They follow the same path and land in the same place.

Skis in the sky
A ski jumper races down a steep chute and leaps into the air. Pulled by gravity, he leaves the chute at high speed. He continues to move forwards through the air as he drops, making a long jump.

Ramp racer

Race a car down a ramp from different heights and see how far and fast it goes! Gravity makes objects move faster the farther they fall.

You will need:

Scissors

Cardboard box with lid

Toy car

Each slot should reach halfway along.

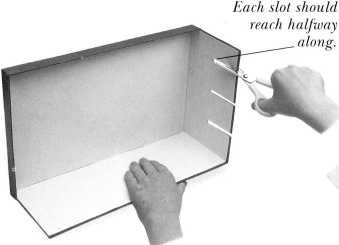

Make the slot half the width of the lid.

Cut into the corner to open out the lid.

1 Cut away most of one end and one side of the cardboard box. Cut three slots in the end that is left.

2 Cut the lid to the same width as the side of the box. Cut a slot in one side near the end. This is your ramp.

Gravity pulls the car down the ramp. It gains speed and travels a short distance.

3 Fit the ramp into the bottom slot of the box. Then release the toy car from the top of the ramp.

4 Fit the ramp into the middle slot and release the car again. This time it moves faster and travels farther.

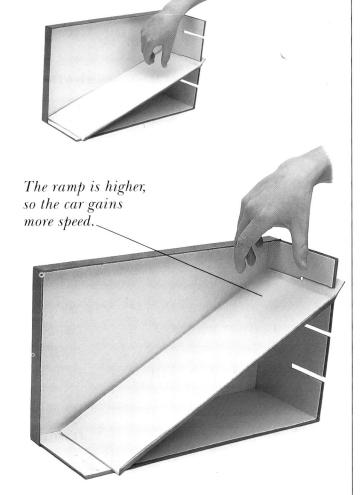

The ramp is higher, so the car gains more speed.

5 Fit the ramp into the top slot. Now the car races down the ramp and travels a long way.

Gravity pulls the car to reach its highest speed when it is released from the greatest height.

Hold on tight!

The cars on this fairground ride have no motors – gravity alone provides the power they need to race around the track. The ride begins with a fast drop down a steep ramp. This gives the cars enough speed for the rest of the ride.

Simple swinger

Set a pendulum swinging and see how each swing takes the same time. What happens if you change the weight and length of the pendulum?

You will need:

Sticky tape

Three large metal nuts

String

Scissors

Watch showing seconds

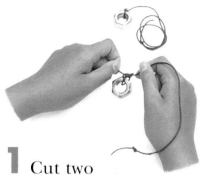

1 Cut two different lengths of string. Tie a metal nut to each string. These are your pendulums. Tape the short one to a support.

2 Set the pendulum swinging. Time each swing from one side to the other and back. Release the pendulum from a greater height and time it again.

Each swing takes the same time, no matter where the swing starts from.

Gravity pulls the end of the pendulum back down as it reaches the top of each swing.

3 Make the pendulum heavier by adding an extra metal nut.

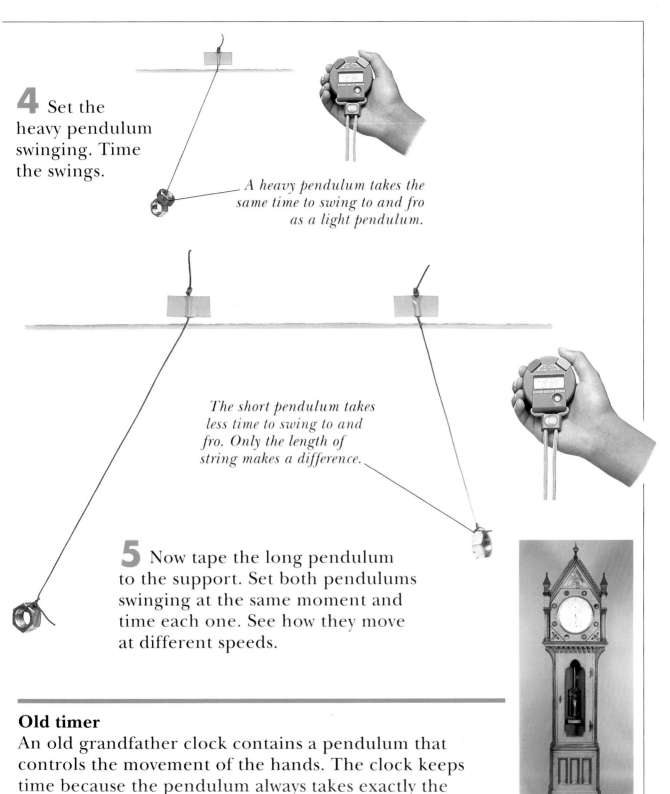

4 Set the heavy pendulum swinging. Time the swings.

A heavy pendulum takes the same time to swing to and fro as a light pendulum.

The short pendulum takes less time to swing to and fro. Only the length of string makes a difference.

5 Now tape the long pendulum to the support. Set both pendulums swinging at the same moment and time each one. See how they move at different speeds.

Old timer
An old grandfather clock contains a pendulum that controls the movement of the hands. The clock keeps time because the pendulum always takes exactly the same time to swing to and fro.

Water clock

Do you know how to measure time with falling water? Build a simple water clock. It works because gravity makes water fall at a regular rate over a period of time.

You will need:

Four paperclips

Plastic cup

Water

Four kebab sticks

Sticky label

Pen

Watch showing seconds

Clear plastic bottle

1 ⚠ Ask an adult to cut the top off the bottle. Then make a small hole near the base of the cup with one of the kebab sticks.

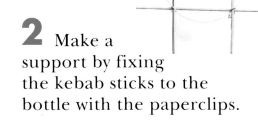

2 Make a support by fixing the kebab sticks to the bottle with the paperclips.

3 Make a mark on the label and stick it to the side of the bottle. Pour water up to the mark.

4 Put the cup in the support. Fill the cup with water. Start timing with the watch as you begin to pour.

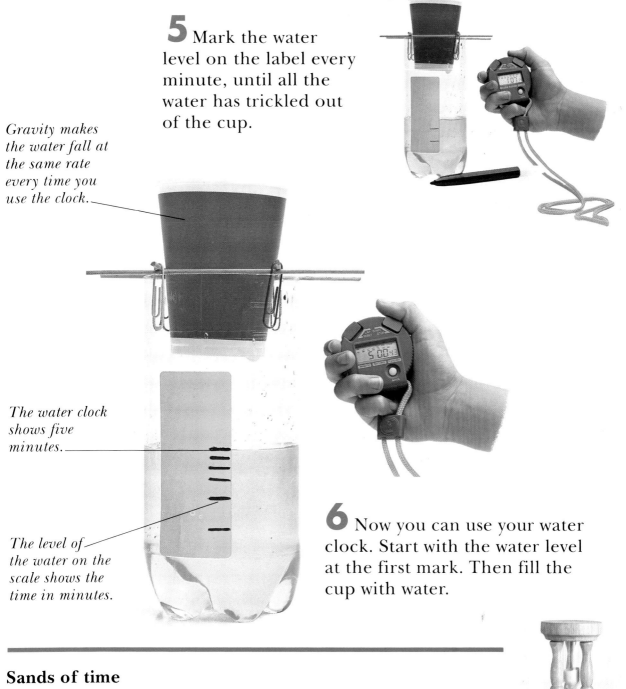

5 Mark the water level on the label every minute, until all the water has trickled out of the cup.

Gravity makes the water fall at the same rate every time you use the clock.

The water clock shows five minutes.

The level of the water on the scale shows the time in minutes.

6 Now you can use your water clock. Start with the water level at the first mark. Then fill the cup with water.

Sands of time

This egg timer measures the time it takes to boil an egg. It contains sand, which always takes three minutes to fall from the top chamber into the bottom chamber. To start the egg timer, you just turn it upside-down.

Balancing act

Gravity seems to pull an object downwards from just one point, its "centre of gravity". Find this to balance an uneven shape on your finger.

You will need:

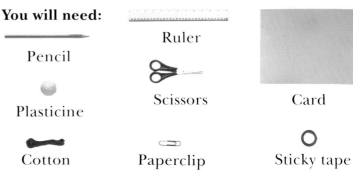

Pencil

Plasticine

Cotton

Ruler

Scissors

Paperclip

Card

Sticky tape

1 Cut out an uneven shape from the card.

Make the holes over a mat.

2 Using the point of the pencil, make two small holes on opposite sides of the shape near the edges.

3 Now make a plumb line. Tie a loop in one end of the cotton and fix a blob of plasticine to the other end.

4 Unbend the paperclip to make a hook. Tape it to the edge of a table. Hang the shape and then the plumb line on the hook.

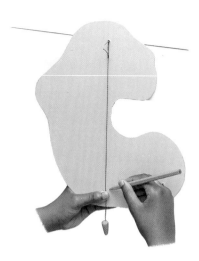

5 When the line stops moving, mark a cross where it lies near the edge of the shape.

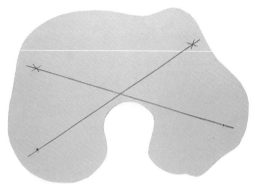

6 Take the shape off the hook and draw a line between the cross and the hole. Hang the shape from the other hole and repeat steps 4 to 6.

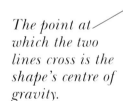

The point at which the two lines cross is the shape's centre of gravity.

Gravity pulls down equally on all parts of the shape around its centre of gravity, so that it balances.

7 Place the shape on your finger at the point where the two lines cross. The shape balances.

On the beam
This gymnast keeps her balance on a narrow beam by making sure her centre of gravity stays directly above the beam.

Clever clown

Make a clown that can balance upside-down on a high wire and never fall off! All you have to do is get the clown's centre of gravity under the wire.

You will need:

String

○○
Two metal nuts

Colouring pens

●
Plasticine

Card

✂
Scissors

Two bottles of water

1 Draw the figure of a clown with outstretched arms on the card. Colour in the clown.

2 Cut out the clown and make a small notch in its nose.

3 Stick a metal nut behind each of the clown's hands with some plasticine.

4 Tie the string to the necks of the bottles. Move the bottles apart to make a high wire.

5 Place the clown on the string so that it rests on the notch in its nose. The clown balances. Push it gently. It swings to and fro, but does not fall off!

Most of the clown's weight is in the heavy metal nuts at the ends of its arms.

Stand firm
A television camera needs to stay steady. It is put on a stand with a heavy base. This gives it a low centre of gravity, so it will not tip over easily.

The clown cannot fall because its centre of gravity, which is under the string, pulls it down on to the string.

Roll up, roll up

Can a wheel roll uphill? It will if you change the wheel's centre of gravity, so that it falls as the wheel rises.

You will need:

Marbles   Round lid   Stiff card

Plasticine   Rubber bands

1 Fit the rubber bands around the lid.

Place the marbles close together.

2 Stick the marbles inside the lid with plasticine.

Make sure the marbles are at the top of the wheel, facing up the ramp.

Gravity pulls the marbles down as low as possible.

The wheel's centre of gravity is in the marbles because they are the heaviest part of the wheel.

3 Fold the card to make a ramp. Put the wheel at the bottom of the ramp.

4 Release the wheel. It rolls up the ramp and stops near the top!

Tip top

This wobbly toy has a heavy base. If you tip it over, its low centre of gravity makes it roll upright again.

Funny flier

Have fun trying to catch a balloon that refuses to fly straight! Its centre of gravity moves around as it flies through the air, making it wobble about.

You will need:

Two balloons

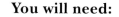

Water

Balloon pump

1 Pour some water into one of the balloons and tie a knot in the neck.

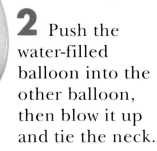

2 Push the water-filled balloon into the other balloon, then blow it up and tie the neck.

The balloon wobbles because its centre of gravity changes as it moves.

The balloon's centre of gravity is in the water-filled balloon.

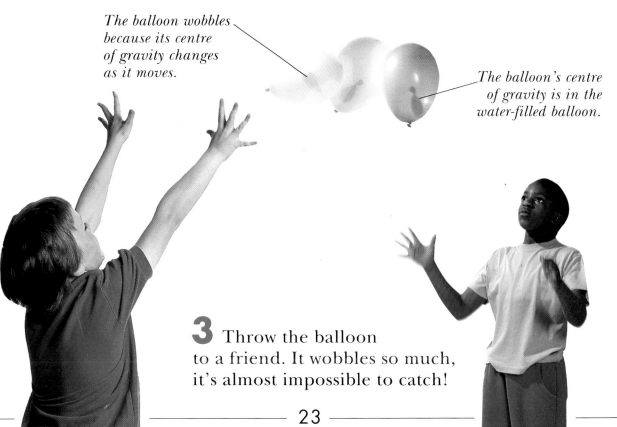

3 Throw the balloon to a friend. It wobbles so much, it's almost impossible to catch!

23

Super balance

Hold something tiny in your hand. It might feel weightless, but gravity gives everything weight. Make a sensitive balance that can detect the weight of even the lightest objects.

You will need:

Cardboard strip   Pin   Ruler

Scissors   Screw   Bendy straw

Pieces of cotton   Empty matchbox   Pen   Plasticine

1 Push some plasticine into the long end of the straw. Then twist the screw into the plasticine.

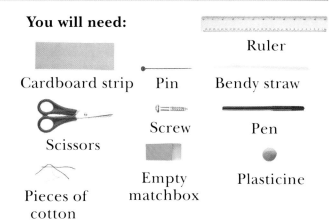

2 Cut a notch in the other end of the straw.

3 ⚠ Push the pin through the straw near the screw.

4 Make a support by cutting the outside part of the matchbox in half.

— 24 —

5 Draw a scale on the cardboard strip. Then bend the strip and stand it behind the notched end of the straw.

Bend the end of the straw, then put the pin on the support.

Adjust the screw until the end of the straw is level with the top mark on the scale.

The cotton makes this end of the balance slightly heavier. Gravity pulls it so that the straw tilts.

6 This is your balance. Gently place a piece of cotton on the end of the balance. See how the straw moves down the scale.

The weight of an object is the force with which gravity pulls on it.

Weight check

Scientists use very sensitive weighing machines to measure small amounts of chemicals and medicines. A weighing machine like this one is so accurate, it can measure weight to a ten-thousandth of a gram.

Weight lifter

The Earth's gravity pulls down on everything, but some forces work against it. See how water pushes up against objects and makes them less heavy.

You will need:

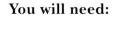

Two paperclips

Scissors

Sticky tape

Water

Plasticine

Tall, clear container

Two full pots

Four rubber bands

Knitting needle

1 Loop a short rubber band around each pot. Unbend the paperclips and hook them under the rubber bands.

Put plasticine on the sharp end of the needle.

Hang one pot inside the container.

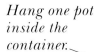

2 Place the knitting needle across the top of the container. Hang both pots from the needle with long rubber bands.

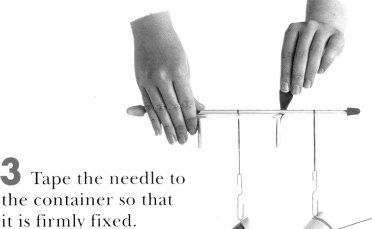

3 Tape the needle to the container so that it is firmly fixed.

Both pots hang at the same height because they weigh the same.

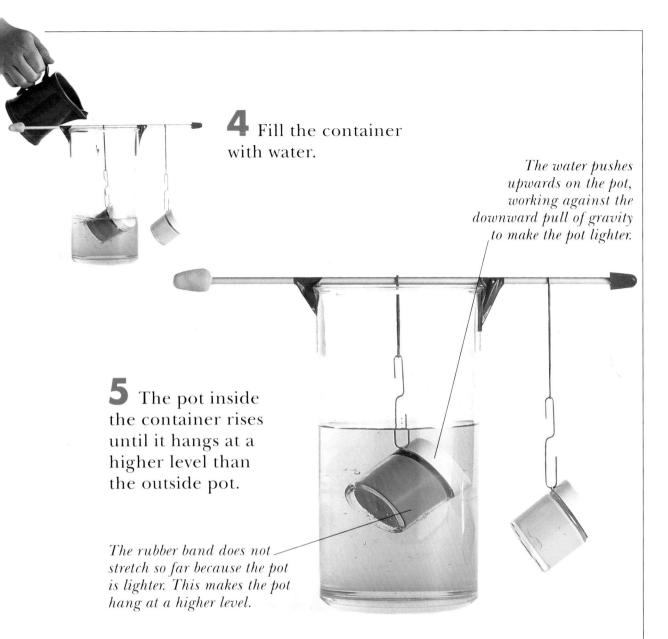

4 Fill the container with water.

The water pushes upwards on the pot, working against the downward pull of gravity to make the pot lighter.

5 The pot inside the container rises until it hangs at a higher level than the outside pot.

The rubber band does not stretch so far because the pot is lighter. This makes the pot hang at a higher level.

Travelling timber

It is hard to move these heavy logs on land. That's why they are moved on water. The water works against the downward pull of gravity, lifting the logs and making them easier to move.

Odd bottle

Can you hold water in a bottle with holes in the bottom? See how air stops it from falling – the water appears to defy gravity!

You will need:

Scissors

Water

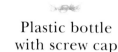

Bowl

Plastic bottle with screw cap

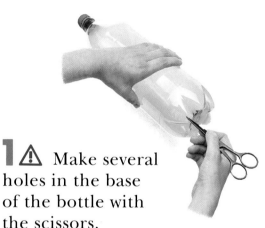

1 ⚠ Make several holes in the base of the bottle with the scissors.

2 Stand the bottle in the bowl and quickly fill it with water. Screw on the cap right away.

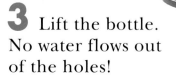

Hold the bottle by the cap and do not squeeze the sides.

3 Lift the bottle. No water flows out of the holes!

Air under the bottle pushes up against the holes. It works against the force of gravity and stops the water from falling.

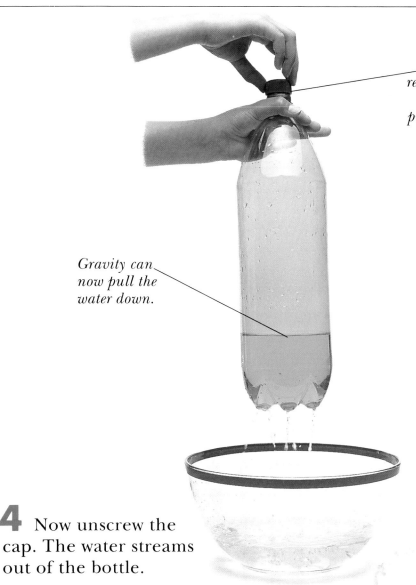

When the cap is removed, air enters the bottle and pushes downwards on the water.

Gravity can now pull the water down.

4 Now unscrew the cap. The water streams out of the bottle.

Clever clinger
A tree frog grips with suction pads on the ends of its fingers and toes. Air pushing on the pads supports the frog as it clings to leaves and stems.

Picture credits
(Picture credits abbreviation key: B=below, C=centre, L=left, R=right, T=top)

Allsport: 6TL, 7TL, 19BR; Bridgeman Art Library: 15BR; J. Allan Cash: 21BL; Colorsport: 11BL; Pete Gardner: 22BL; The Image Bank/Guido A. Rossi: 27BR; Frank Lane/HD Brand: 29BR; NASA/Science Photo Library: 6TR, 7TR; Planet Earth Pictures/Mike Coltman: 7CR; Pictor International: 9BR, 13BR; Tim Ridley: 7BL, 17BR; Science Photo Library/David Leah: 25BR

Picture research Clive Webster

Science consultant Jack Challoner

Additional photography Dave King and Tim Ridley

Dorling Kindersley would like to thank Jenny Vaughan for editorial assistance; Basil Snook for supplying toys; Mrs Bradbury, Mr Millington, the staff and children of Allfarthing Junior School, Wandsworth, especially Hannah Carey, Richard Clenshaw, Nadeen Flower, Alex MacDougald, Keisha McLeod, Kemi Owoturo, Casston Rogers-Brown, Ben Sells, Cheryl Smith, and Michael Spencer.